TRANSLATED

Translated Language Learning

The Diaries of Adam and Eve
亚当和夏娃日记

Mark Twain
马克·吐温

English /普通话

Copyright © 2023 Tranzlaty
All rights reserved.
Published by Tranzlaty
ISBN: 978-1-83566-184-0
Original texts by Mark Twain:
Extracts from Adam's Diary: Translated from the Original MS
First published in The Niagara Book 1893
Eve's Diary
First published in Harper's Bazaar 1905
Illustrated by Lester Ralph
www.tranzlaty.com

- Extracts from Adam's Diary -
- 摘自亚当日记 –

I had translated a portion of this diary some years ago
几年前,我翻译了这本日记的一部分
a friend of mine printed a few copies of the text
我的一个朋友打印了几本文字
the text was in an incomplete form
文本形式不完整
but the public never got to see those texts
但公众从未看到过这些文字。
Since then I have deciphered some more of Adam's hieroglyphics
从那以后,我破译了更多的亚当象形文字。
he has now become sufficiently important as a public character
他现在作为一个公众人物已经变得足够重要
and I think this publication can now be justified
我认为这个出版物现在可以证明是合理的
Mark Twain
马克·吐温

MONDAY - 星期一
This new creature with the long hair is constantly in the way
这个长着长发的新生物不断挡路
It is always hanging around and following me about
它总是在徘徊和跟随我
I don't like this
我不喜欢这样
I am not used to company
我不习惯陪伴
I wish it would stay with the other animals
我希望它能和其他动物在一起

Cloudy to-day, wind in the east
今天多云,东风

I think we shall have rain
我想我们会下雨的
Where did I get that word?
我从哪里得到这个词？
I remember now
我现在记得
the new creature uses that word
新生物使用这个词

TUESDAY - 星期二
I've been examining the great waterfall
我一直在研究大瀑布
the great waterfall is the finest thing on the estate, I think
大瀑布是庄园里最好的东西，我认为
The new creature calls it Niagara Falls
新生物称之为尼亚加拉大瀑布
why does it call it Niagara falls?
为什么叫它尼亚加拉大瀑布？
I am sure I do not know
我确定我不知道
it says the waterfall looks like Niagara Falls
它说瀑布看起来像尼亚加拉大瀑布
That is not a reason
这不是理由
it is mere waywardness and imbecility
这只是任性和愚蠢
I get no chance to name anything myself
我没有机会自己命名任何东西
The new creature names everything that comes along
新生物命名了出现的一切
I don't even get time to protest
我什至没有时间抗议
the same pretext is always offered
总是提供相同的借口
"it looks like the thing"
"看起来很像"
There is the dodo, for instance

例如，有渡渡鸟

it says the moment one looks at it one sees the animal "looks like a dodo"
它说，当人们看到它的那一刻，他看到动物"**看起来像一只渡渡鸟**"

It will have to keep that name, no doubt
毫无疑问，它必须保留这个名字

It wearies me to fret about it
让我烦恼

and it does no good to worry about it, anyway
无论如何，担心它没有任何好处

Dodo! It looks no more like a dodo than I do
渡渡鸟！它看起来并不比我更像渡渡鸟

WEDNESDAY - 星期三
I built myself a shelter against the rain
我为自己建了一个避雨棚

but I could not have it to myself in peace
但我不能平静地拥有自己

The new creature intruded
新生物入侵

I tried to put it out
我试图把它拿出来

but it shed water out of the holes it looks with
但它从它看起来的洞里流出水

it wiped the water away with the back of its paws
它用爪子的后背把水擦掉了

and it made a noise like the animals do when they are in distress
它发出的声音就像动物遇险时的声音一样。

I wish it would not talk
我希望它不会说话

it is always talking
它总是在说话

That sounds like a cheap fling at the poor creature
这听起来像是对可怜的生物的廉价投掷

but I do not mean it to sound like a slur

但我不是故意听起来像诽谤
I have never heard the human voice before
我以前从未听过人的声音
for me it is a new and strange sound
对我来说,这是一种新奇而奇怪的声音
and this sound intrudes itself upon the solemn hush of these dreaming solitudes
而这声音侵入了这些梦幻孤独的庄严寂静
it offends my ear and seems a false note
它冒犯了我的耳朵,似乎是一个假音符
And this new sound is so close to me
而这个新声音离我如此之近
it is right at my shoulder, right at my ear
它就在我的肩膀上,就在我耳边
first on one side and then on the other
先在一侧,然后在另一侧
I am used only to sounds that are at a distance from me
我只习惯于离我很远的声音

FRIDAY - 星期五
The naming goes recklessly on, in spite of anything I can do
命名不计后果地进行,尽管我能做任何事情
I had a very good name for the estate: Garden of Eden
我对庄园有一个非常好的名字:伊甸园
it was musical and pretty
它很有音乐感,很漂亮
Privately, I continue to call it that
私下里,我继续这样称呼它
but I don't call it that in public anymore
但我不再在公共场合这么称呼它了
The new creature says it is all woods and rocks and scenery
新生物说这都是树林、岩石和风景
therefore it has no resemblance to a garden, it says
因此,它与花园没有相似之处,它说
it says it looks like a park
它说它看起来像一个公园

it says it does not look like anything but a park
它说它看起来不像一个公园
without consulting me, it decided to rename the garden
在没有咨询我的情况下,它决定重命名花园
now it's called Niagara falls park
现在它被称为尼亚加拉大瀑布公园
it is becoming too much for me
对我来说变得太多了
And there is already a sign up
并且已经有注册
"Keep off the grass"
"远离草地"
My life is not as happy as it was
我的生活不像以前那么幸福了

SATURDAY - 星期六
The new creature eats too much fruit
新生物吃了太多水果
We may well run short of fruit quite soon
我们可能很快就会缺水果
"we", again. That is one of its words
"我们",再次。这是它的话之一
I've heard the word so many times
这个词我听过很多次
and now it's one of my words too
现在这也是我的话之一

There is a good deal of fog this morning
今天早上有很多雾
I do not go out in the fog
我不在雾中出去
The new creature always goes out in the fog
新生物总是在迷雾中熄灭
It goes out in all weathers
它在各种天气下都熄灭
it stumps around outside with its muddy feet and talks
它用泥泞的脚在外面跟跟跄跄地说话

It used to be so pleasant and quiet here
这里曾经如此宜人而安静

SUNDAY - 星期日
This day is getting to be more and more trying
这一天越来越艰难
last November we made this day a day of rest
去年11月，我们把这一天定为休息日。
I already had six days of rest per week
我已经每周休息六天了
This morning I found the new creature at the forbidden tree
今天早上我在禁树上发现了这个新生物
it was trying to clod apples out of that forbidden tree
它试图从那棵禁树上挖出苹果

MONDAY - 星期一
The new creature says its name is Eve
新生物说它的名字是夏娃
That is all right
没关系
I have no objections to it being called Eve
我不反对它被称为夏娃
it says I should call Eve when I want it to come
它说我应该在我想来的时候打电话给夏娃
I said that would be superfluous
我说那将是多余的
The word evidently raised me in its respect
这个词显然使我感到尊重
it is indeed a large and good word
这确实是一个大而好词
this word will be worth repeating
这个词值得重复
It says it is not an "it"
它说它不是"它"
it says it is a "She"
它说这是一个"她"
This is probably doubtful

这可能是值得怀疑的
but it is all the same to me
但对我来说都是一样的
whatever she is wouldn't matter if she didn't talk so much
不管她是什么，如果她不那么说话都无所谓

TUESDAY - 星期二
She has littered the whole estate with execrable names and offensive signs:
她在整个庄园里散落着可执行的名字和令人反感的标志：
"this way to the whirlpool"
"这条路去漩涡"
"this way to goat island"
"这条路去山羊岛"
"cave of the winds this way"
《风之洞》
She says this park would make a tidy summer resort
她说这个公园会成为一个整洁的避暑胜地。
but summer resorts are not at all customary
但避暑胜地根本不习惯
"Summer resort" - another invention of hers
"避暑胜地"——她的另一项发明
just words without any meaning
只是没有任何意义的文字
What is a summer resort?
什么是避暑胜地？
But it is best not to ask her
但最好不要问她
she has so much energy for explaining
她有那么多精力去解释

FRIDAY - 星期五
She has taken to beseeching me to stop going over the Falls
她恳求我不要再越过瀑布了
What harm does it do?
它有什么危害？
Says it makes her shudder

- 7 -

说这让她不寒而栗
I wonder why it makes her shudder
我想知道为什么这让她不寒而栗
I have always jumped down from the waterfalls
我总是从瀑布上跳下来
I liked the plunge and the excitement
我喜欢跳水和兴奋
and I liked the coolness of the water
我喜欢水的凉爽
I supposed it was what the Falls were for
我以为这就是瀑布的用途
They have no other use that I can see
他们没有我能看到的其他用途
and they must have been made for something
它们一定是为了某事而生的
She says they were only made for scenery
她说它们只是为了风景而生的
like the rhinoceros and the mastodon
像犀牛和乳齿象
I went over the Falls in a barrel
我在一个桶里越过瀑布
but that was not satisfactory to her
但这对她来说并不满意
I Went over the falls in a tub
我在浴缸里越过瀑布
it was still not satisfactory
还是不尽如人意
I swam the Whirlpool and the Rapids in a fig-leaf suit
我穿着遮羞布套装在漩涡和急流中游泳
my suit got very damaged
我的西装损坏得很厉害
so I had to listen to tedious complaints about my extravagance
所以我不得不听关于我奢侈的乏味抱怨
I am too hampered here
我在这里太受阻了
What I need is change of scenery

我需要的是风景的变化

SATURDAY - 星期六

I escaped last Tuesday night and travelled two days
我上周二晚上逃脱了，旅行了两天
I built another shelter in a secluded place
我在一个僻静的地方建造了另一个避难所
and I obliterated my tracks as well as I could
我尽可能地抹去了我的踪迹
but she hunted me out with the aid of one of her beasts
但她在她的一只野兽的帮助下猎杀了我
a beast which she has tamed and calls a wolf
被她驯服并称为狼的野兽
she came making that pitiful noise again
她又来了，发出那种可怜的声音
and she was shedding that water out of the places she looks with
她正在把水从她看的地方流出来
I was obliged to return with her
我不得不和她一起回去
but I will emigrate again, when an occasion presents itself
但我会再次移民，当一个机会出现时

She engages herself in many foolish things
她从事许多愚蠢的事情
she's trying to understand why the lions and tigers eat grass and flowers
她试图理解为什么狮子和老虎吃草和花。
she says their teeth would indicate that they were intended to eat each other
她说他们的牙齿表明他们打算吃掉对方。
This is a foolish idea
这是一个愚蠢的想法
to do that they would have to kill each other
要做到这一点，他们将不得不互相残杀
as I understand it that would introduce what is called

"death"
据我了解,这将引入所谓的"死亡"
and I have been told that death has not yet entered the Park
有人告诉我,死亡还没有进入公园
on some accounts that is a pity
在某些方面,这很可惜

SUNDAY - rested
周日 - 休息

MONDAY - 星期一
I believe I see what the week is for
我相信我明白本周是为了什么
it is to give time to rest up from the weariness of Sunday
这是为了给时间从星期天的疲惫中休息
It seems a good idea
这似乎是个好主意

She has been climbing that tree again
她又爬上了那棵树
I clodded her out of it
我把她从里面拽了出来
She said nobody was looking
她说没人看
she seems to consider that a sufficient justification
她似乎认为这是一个充分的理由
but it is no justification for chancing a dangerous thing
但这不是追捕危险事物的理由
I told her it was no justification for what she did
我告诉她,她的所作所为没有理由。
The word "justification" moved her admiration
"辩解"二字感动了她的钦佩
she seemed to envy me a little, I thought
她似乎有点羡慕我,我想
It is a good word
这是一个好词
I shall use the word more often
我将更频繁地使用这个词

THURSDAY - 星期四
She told me she was made out of one of my ribs
她告诉我她是用我的一根肋骨做的
I somewhat doubt what she says
我有点怀疑她说的话
I don't seem to be missing a rib
我似乎没有缺少一根肋骨
and I can't imagine how she would have been made from my rib
我无法想象她是如何用我的肋骨制成的
She is making a great fuss about the buzzard
她对秃鹰大惊小怪
she says his stomach does not agree with the grass
她说他的肚子与草不符
she is afraid she can't raise the buzzard
她怕自己养不出秃鹰
she thinks it was intended to live on decayed flesh
她认为这是为了生活在腐烂的肉体上
The buzzard must get along the best it can with what is provided
秃鹰必须与所提供的东西相处得最好
We cannot overturn the whole scheme to accommodate the buzzard
我们不能推翻整个计划来容纳秃鹰

SATURDAY - 星期六
She fell in the pond while she was looking at herself in it
她掉进了池塘里,而她看着池塘里的自己。
she is always looking at herself
她总是在看着自己
She was nearly strangled by the water
她差点被水勒死
and she said it was most uncomfortable
她说这是最不舒服的
This made her sorry for the creatures which live in the water
这让她为生活在水中的生物感到难过。
the creatures which she calls fish

她称之为鱼的生物

she continues to fasten names on to things that don't need them
她继续将名字固定在不需要它们的东西上。

the don't come when they are called by those names
当他们被这些名字称呼时，不要来

but this is a matter of no consequence to her
但这对她来说无关紧要

she is such a numbskull
她真是个麻木的头骨

she took a lot of the fish out of the water last night
她昨晚从水里拿了很多鱼

and then she brought them into the house
然后她把他们带进了房子

she put them in my bed so they would be warm
她把它们放在我的床上，这样它们就会很温暖

but they don't seem any happier than where they were before
但他们似乎并不比以前更快乐。

all I can see is that they are quieter
我只能看到他们更安静

When night comes I shall throw them out again
当夜幕降临时，我会再次把它们扔出去

I will not sleep with these fish in my bed again
我不会再和这些鱼一起睡在我的床上了

I find lying unclothed among them clammy and unpleasant
我发现躺在他们中间不穿衣服又湿又不愉快

SUNDAY - rested
周日 - 休息

TUESDAY - 星期二

She has made friends with a snake
她和一条蛇交了朋友

The other animals are glad that she is friends with the snake
其他动物很高兴她是蛇的朋友

because she was always experimenting with the other animals
因为她总是在用其他动物做实验
and she was always bothering the other animals
她总是打扰其他动物
and I am also glad she is friends with the snake
我也很高兴她和蛇是朋友
because the snake talks
因为蛇会说话
now she spends more time talking with the snake instead of me
现在她花更多的时间与蛇交谈，而不是我
and this enables me to get a rest
这使我能够得到休息

FRIDAY - 星期五
She says the snake advises her to try the fruit of the forbidden tree
她说蛇建议她尝试禁树的果实
and she says the result will be a great and fine and noble education
她说，结果将是伟大、美好和高尚的教育。
I told her there would be another result, too
我告诉她也会有另一个结果
eating from the tree would introduce death into the world
吃树会把死亡引入世界
telling her the fruit would bring death into the world was a mistake
告诉她果子会给世界带来死亡是一个错误
it would have been better to keep the remark to myself
最好把这句话留给自己
telling her about death gave her another idea
告诉她关于死亡的事情给了她另一个想法
she could save the sick buzzard
她可以拯救生病的秃鹰
and she could furnish fresh meat to the despondent lions

and tigers
她可以为沮丧的狮子和老虎提供新鲜的肉
I advised her to keep away from the tree
我劝她离树远点
She said she wouldn't keep away from the tree
她说她不会远离这棵树
I foresee trouble and I will emigrate
我预见到麻烦，我会移民

WEDNESDAY - 星期三
I have had an eventful time since I escaped
自从我逃脱以来，我度过了一段多事的时光
I escaped on the night she ate from the tree
我在她从树上吃东西的那天晚上逃脱了
and I rode a horse all night as fast as he could go
我整夜骑着马，他走得越快越快
I hoped to get out of the park and hide in some other country
我希望走出公园，躲到其他国家
I hoped I would get away before the trouble began
我希望我能在麻烦开始之前逃脱
but my plans were not to be
但我的计划不是
About an hour after sunup I was riding through a flowery plain
日出后大约一个小时，我骑车穿过一片鲜花盛开的平原
thousands of animals were grazing and slumbering
数以千计的动物在吃草和沉睡
and the young animals were playing with each other
小动物们在互相玩耍
all of a sudden they broke into a tempest of frightful noises
突然间，他们闯入了一场可怕的噪音风暴中
and in one moment the plain was in a frantic commotion
一瞬间，平原上一片疯狂的骚动
every beast was destroying its neighbour
每只野兽都在摧毁它的邻居

I knew what it meant; Eve had eaten that fruit
我知道这意味着什么;夏娃吃了那个果子

death had come into the world
死亡来到了这个世界

The tigers ate my horse
老虎吃了我的马

they payed no attention when I ordered them to desist
当我命令他们停止时,他们没有理会

they would even have eaten me if I had stayed
如果我留下来,他们甚至会吃掉我

I found this place outside the park
我在公园外找到了这个地方

I was fairly comfortable for a few days
我住几天还算舒服

but she has found my hiding place
但她找到了我的藏身之处

and she has named the place Tonawanda
她将这个地方命名为托纳旺达

she says it looks like Tonawanda
她说看起来像托纳旺达

In fact, I was not sorry she came
其实我并不后悔她来了

there are but meagre pickings here
这里只有很少的采摘

and she brought some of those apples
她带来了一些苹果

I was so hungry that I to eat them
我太饿了,我想吃它们

eating those apples was against my principles
吃那些苹果违背了我的原则

but I find that principles have no real force except when one is well fed
但我发现原则没有真正的力量,除非一个人吃饱了

She came curtained in boughs and bunches of leaves
她披着树枝和一束树叶的窗帘

I asked her what she meant by such nonsense
我问她这种胡说八道是什么意思
I snatched the leaves from her
我从她手里抢过叶子
and threw her coverings onto the ground
然后把她的被子扔在地上
she tittered and blushed when I did this
当我这样做时,她会叽叽喳喳,脸红
I had never seen a person titter and blush before
我以前从未见过一个人和脸红
her manner seemed to be unbecoming and idiotic
她的态度似乎不合时宜,很白痴
but she said I would soon know how it felt
但她说我很快就会知道那是什么感觉
in this she was correct
在这一点上她是对的
I have come to understand the feeling of shame
我开始理解羞耻感

Hungry as I was, I laid down the apple half eaten
我饿了,把苹果吃了一半放下
it was certainly the best apple I ever saw
这当然是我见过的最好的苹果
it was as especially good apple, considering the lateness of the season
考虑到季节的迟到,它就像特别好的苹果一样
and I covered myself in the discarded boughs and branches
我把自己盖在废弃的树枝和树枝上
then I spoke to her with some severity
然后我有些严厉地和她说话
I ordered her to go and get some more apples
我命令她再去拿一些苹果
and I told her not make such a spectacle of herself
我告诉她不要把自己弄成这样的奇观
She did as I told her
她按照我告诉她的做了
then we crept down to where the wild beasts bad battled

然后我们蹑手蹑脚地来到野兽巴德战斗的地方
and we collected some of their furs
我们收集了一些他们的毛皮
I made her patch together a couple of suits proper for public occasions
我给她整理了几套适合公共场合的西装
They are uncomfortable, it is true
他们不舒服,这是真的
but this clothing we now wear is stylish
但是我们现在穿的这件衣服很时尚
and that is the main point about clothes
这就是关于衣服的要点

I find she is a good companion to have
我发现她是一个很好的伴侣
I would be lonesome and depressed without her
没有她,我会很寂寞和沮丧
if I didn't have her I wouldn't have anyone
如果我没有她,我就不会有任何人
but she says it is ordered that we work for our living from now on
但她说,从现在开始,我们命令我们为生活而工作。
She will be useful in dividing up the work
她将在划分工作方面发挥作用
I will superintend over the work we do
我将监督我们所做的工作

Ten Days Later
十天后

She accuses me of being the cause of our disaster!
她指责我是造成我们灾难的原因!
She says the Serpent assured her that the forbidden fruit was not apples
她说蛇向她保证,禁果不是苹果。
and she says this with apparent sincerity and truth
她说这句话时带着明显的真诚和真实

she says they weren't apples, but instead that they were chestnuts
她说它们不是苹果，而是栗子。
I said I was innocent since I had not eaten any chestnuts
我说我是无辜的，因为我没有吃过任何栗子
but the Serpent informed her that "chestnut" could also have a figurative meaning
但蛇告诉她，"栗子"也可以有比喻的意思
she says a chestnut can be an aged and mouldy joke
她说栗子可能是一个陈年和发霉的笑话
I turned pale at this definition
我对这个定义变得苍白
because I have made many jokes to pass the weary time
因为我开了很多玩笑来打发疲惫的时间
and some of them my jokes could have been of the chestnut variety
其中一些我的笑话可能是栗子品种
but I had honestly supposed that they were new jokes when I made them
但老实说，当我制作它们时，我以为它们是新笑话
She asked me if I had made any jokes just at the time of the catastrophe
她问我是否在灾难发生时开过什么玩笑。
I was obliged to admit that I had made a joke to myself
我不得不承认我自嘲地开了个玩笑。
although I did not make the joke aloud
虽然我没有大声开玩笑
this was the joke I was thinking to myself:
这是我对自己开的玩笑：
I was thinking about the waterfalls
我在想瀑布
"How wonderful it is to see that vast body of water tumble down there!"
"看到那片浩瀚的海水滚落在那里，真是太好了！"
Then in an instant a bright thought flashed into my head
然后一瞬间，一个明亮的念头闪过我的脑海。
"It would be a great deal more wonderful to see the water

tumble up the waterfall!"
"如果能看到瀑布上的水翻滚,那就太好了!"
I was just about to die from laughing when all nature broke loose
我正要笑死时,所有的大自然都崩溃了。
and I had to flee for my life
我不得不逃命
"now you see" she said triumphantly
"现在你明白了"她得意洋洋地说。
"the Serpent mentioned that very jest"
"蛇提到了那个笑话"
"he called it the First Chestnut"
"他称它为第一栗子"
"and he said it was coeval with the creation"
"他说这与创作是同时代的"
Alas, I am indeed to blame
唉,我确实是罪魁祸首
I wish that I were not so witty
我希望我不要那么机智
I wish that I had never had that radiant thought!
我希望我从来没有过那种光芒四射的想法!

Next Year
明年

We have named it Cain
我们将其命名为该隐
She caught it while I was up country trapping on the North Shore of the Erie
当我在伊利河北岸进行乡村陷阱时,她抓住了它
she caught it in the timber a couple of miles from our dug-out
她在离我们挖出的几英里远的树林里抓住了它
or it might have been four miles
或者可能是四英里
she isn't certain how far it was
她不确定它有多远

It resembles us in some ways
它在某些方面与我们相似

it may even be a relation to us
它甚至可能与我们有关

That is what she thinks
她就是这么想的

but this is an error, in my judgement
但在我看来，这是一个错误

The difference in size suggests it is a new kind of animal
大小的差异表明它是一种新型动物

it is perhaps a fish
也许是一条鱼

though when I put it in the water it sank
虽然当我把它放在水里时它沉没了

and she plunged in and snatched it out of the water
她一头扎进去，把它从水里抢了出来。

so there was no opportunity for the experiment to determine the matter
所以实验没有机会确定此事

I still think it is a fish
我仍然认为它是一条鱼

but she is indifferent about what it is
但她对它是什么无动于衷

and she will not let me have it to try
她不会让我尝试

I do not understand this
我不明白这一点

The coming of the creature seems to have changed her whole nature
这个生物的到来似乎改变了她的整个本性。

it has made her unreasonable about experiments
这让她对实验不讲道理

She thinks more of it than she does of any of the other animals
她比任何其他动物都想得更多

but she is not able to explain why she likes it so much
但她无法解释为什么她这么喜欢它

Her mind is disordered
她的思想紊乱了
everything shows how disordered her mind is
一切都表明她的思想是多么紊乱
Sometimes she carries the fish in her arms half the night
有时她半夜把鱼抱在怀里
she looks after the fish when it complains
当鱼抱怨时，她会照顾它
I think it complains because it wants to get to the water
我认为它抱怨是因为它想下水
At such times the water comes out of the places that she looks out of
在这种时候，水从她看的地方流出来
and she pats the fish on the back and makes soft sounds with her mouth
她拍拍鱼的背，用嘴发出柔和的声音
she betrays sorrow and solicitude in a hundred ways
她以一百种方式出卖悲伤和关怀
I have never seen her do like this with any other fish
我从未见过她对任何其他鱼这样做
and her actions towards the fish trouble me greatly
她对鱼的行为让我非常困扰
She used to carry the young tigers around like she does with the fish
她曾经像对待鱼一样带着幼虎到处走动。
and she used play with the tigers before we lost our property
在我们失去财产之前，她和老虎队一起玩
but with the tigers she was only playing with them
但和老虎队在一起，她只是和他们一起玩
she never worried about them when their dinner disagreed with them
当他们的晚餐与他们不一致时，她从不担心他们

SUNDAY - 星期日

She doesn't work Sundays
她星期天不工作
but she lies around all tired out
但她躺在身边，疲惫不堪
and she likes to have the fish wallow over her
她喜欢让鱼在她身上打滚
she makes foolish noises to amuse the fish
她发出愚蠢的声音来逗鱼
and she pretends to chew its paws
她假装咬它的爪子
the makes the fish laugh
让鱼儿发笑
I have not seen a fish before that could laugh
我以前没有见过会笑的鱼
This makes me doubt whether it really is a fish
这让我怀疑它是否真的是一条鱼
I have come to like Sunday myself
我自己也喜欢星期天
Superintending all the week tires a body so
监督整个星期都会让身体疲惫不堪，所以
There ought to be more Sundays
应该有更多的星期天
In the old days Sundays were tough
在过去，星期天很艰难
but now Sundays are very handy to have
但现在星期天非常方便

WEDNESDAY - 星期三

It isn't a fish
它不是鱼
I cannot quite make out what it is
我不太清楚它是什么
It makes curious and devilish noises when not satisfied
不满意时会发出好奇和恶魔般的声音
and it says "goo-goo" when it is satisfied
满意时说"咕"

It is not one of us, for it doesn't walk
它不是我們中的一員，因為它不會走路。

it is not a bird, for it doesn't fly
它不是鸟，因为它不会飞

it is not a frog, for it doesn't hop
它不是青蛙，因为它不会跳

it is not a snake, for it doesn't crawl
它不是蛇，因为它不会爬行

I feel sure it is not a fish
我确信它不是鱼

but I cannot get a chance to find out whether it can swim or not
但我没有机会知道它是否会游泳

It merely lies around, mostly on its back, with its feet up
它只是躺着，大部分是仰卧着，双脚向上

I have not seen any other animal do that before
我以前从未见过任何其他动物这样做

I said I believed it was an enigma
我说我相信这是一个谜

but she only admired the word without understanding it
但她只是欣赏这个词而不理解它

In my judgement it is either an enigma or some kind of a bug
在我看来，它要么是一个谜，要么是一个错误

If it dies, I will take it apart and see what its arrangements are
如果它死了，我会把它拆开，看看它的安排是什么

I never had a thing perplex me so much
我从来没有一件事让我如此困惑

Three Months Later
三个月后

it is only getting more perplexing, instead of less
它只会变得越来越令人困惑,而不是更少

I sleep but little
我睡得很少

it has ceased from lying around
它已经不再躺着了

it goes about on its four legs now
它现在用四条腿走动

Yet it differs from the other four-legged animals
然而,它与其他四足动物不同

its front legs are unusually short
它的前腿异常短

this causes the main part of its body to stick up uncomfortably high
这导致其身体的主要部分不舒服地高高地翘起

and this is not attractive
这没有吸引力

It is built much as we are
它的建造方式与我们一样

but its method of travelling shows that it is not of our breed
但它的旅行方式表明它不属于我们的品种

The short front legs and long hind ones indicate that it is of the kangaroo family
短的前腿和长长的后腿表明它是袋鼠科的

but it is a marked variation of the species
但它是该物种的显着变异

the true kangaroo hops, but this one never does
真正的袋鼠跳,但这个从来没有

Still, it is a curious and interesting variety
尽管如此,它仍然是一个好奇而有趣的品种

and it has not been catalogued before
并且以前没有编目过

As I discovered it, I feel justified in securing the credit of the discovery
当我发现它时,我觉得有理由确保发现的功劳

and I shall be the one to attach my name to it
我将是那个附上我的名字的人
so I have called it Kangaroorum Adamiensis
所以我称它为袋鼠阿达米恩斯

It must have been a young one when it came
它来的时候一定是个年轻的人
because it has grown exceedingly since it came
因为它自到来以来已经非常增长
It must be five times as big, now, as it was then
它现在一定是当时的五倍大
when discontented it can make twenty-two to thirty-eight times the noise it made at first
当不满时，它可以发出二十二到三十八倍于最初发出的噪音
Coercion does not modify this
胁迫不会修改这一点
if anything, coercion has the contrary effect
如果有的话，胁迫具有相反的效果
For this reason I discontinued the system
出于这个原因，我停止了该系统
She reconciles it by persuasion
她通过说服调和了它
and she gives it things which she had previously told it she wouldn't give it
她给了它她以前告诉它她不会给的东西
As already observed, I was not at home when it first came
正如已经观察到的，当它第一次出现时我不在家
and she told me she found it in the woods
她告诉我她在树林里找到了它。
It seems odd that it should be the only one
奇怪的是，它应该是唯一的一个
yet it must be the only one
但它一定是唯一的
I have worn myself out trying to find another one
我已经疲惫不堪地试图找到另一个
if I had another one in my collection I could study it better
如果我的收藏中还有另一个，我可以更好地研究它

and then this one would have one of its kind to play with
然后这个会有一个这样的玩

surely, then it would be quieter
当然，那会更安静

and then we could tame it more easily
然后我们可以更容易地驯服它

But I find none, nor any vestige of any
但我没有发现，也没有任何痕迹

and strangest of all, I have found no tracks
最奇怪的是，我没有找到任何踪迹

It has to live on the ground
它必须生活在地面上

it cannot help itself
它无法自拔

therefore, how does it get about without leaving a track?
因此，如何在不离开轨道的情况下发挥作用？

I have set a dozen traps
我设置了十几个陷阱

but the traps do no good
但陷阱没有好处

I catch all the small animals except that one
我抓了所有的小动物，除了那只

animals that merely go into the trap out of curiosity
只是出于好奇而进入陷阱的动物

I think they go to see what the milk is there for
我想他们去看看牛奶是干什么用的

but they never drink this milk
但他们从不喝这种牛奶

Three Months Later
三个月后

The kangaroo still continues to grow
袋鼠仍在继续生长

this continual growth is very strange and perplexing
这种持续的增长是非常奇怪和困惑的

I never knew any animal to spend so much time growing
我从来不知道有哪一种动物会花这么多时间成长

It has fur on its head now, but not like kangaroo fur
它现在头上有皮毛,但不像袋鼠皮毛

it's exactly like our hair, but finer and softer
它和我们的头发一模一样,但更细更柔软

and instead of being black its fur is red
它的皮毛不是黑色的,而是红色的

I am like to lose my mind over this zoological freak
我想对这个动物学怪胎失去理智

the capricious and harassing developments are unclassifiable
反复无常和骚扰性的事态发展是无法分类的

If only I could catch another one
要是我能再抓到一只就好了

but it is hopeless trying to find another
但试图找到另一个是没有希望的

I have to accept that it is a new variety
我必须接受这是一个新品种

it is the only sample, this is plain to see
这是唯一的样本,这是显而易见的

But I caught a true kangaroo and brought it in
但我抓了一只真正的袋鼠并把它带了进来

I thought that this one might be lonesome
我以为这个可能很寂寞

so it might prefer to have a kangaroo for company
所以它可能更喜欢有一只袋鼠作伴

otherwise it would have no kin at all
否则它根本没有亲属

and it would have no animal that it could feel a nearness to
它不会有动物可以感觉到接近

this way it might get sympathy for its forlorn condition among strangers
这样，它可能会在陌生人中对其凄凉状况表示同情
strangers who do not know its ways or habits
不知道其方式或习惯的陌生人
strangers who do not know how to make it feel that it is among friends
不知道如何让人感觉在朋友之间的陌生人
but it was a mistake
但这是一个错误
it went into terrible fits at the sight of the kangaroo
一看到袋鼠就变得很糟糕
I am convinced it had never seen a kangaroo before
我确信它以前从未见过袋鼠
I pity the poor noisy little animal
我可怜可怜的吵闹的小动物
but there is nothing I can do to make it happy
但我无能为力让它快乐
I would like to tame it, but that is out of the question
我想驯服它，但这是不可能的
the more I try, the worse I seem to make it
我尝试的越多，我似乎做得越糟糕
It grieves me to the heart to see it in its little storms of sorrow and passion
看到它在悲伤和激情的小风暴中，我感到非常悲伤
I wanted to let it go, but she wouldn't hear of it
我想放手，但她听不到
That seemed cruel and not like her
这看起来很残忍，不像她
and yet she may be right
然而她可能是对的
It might be lonelier than ever
它可能比以往任何时候都更孤独
if I cannot find another one, how could it not be lonely?
如果找不到另一个，怎么能不寂寞？

Five Months Later
五个月后

It is not a kangaroo
它不是袋鼠

holding her fingers it goes a few steps on its hind legs
握着她的手指,它的后腿走了几步

and then it falls down again
然后它又掉下来了

so it is probably some kind of a bear
所以它可能是某种熊

and yet it has no tail, as yet
然而它还没有尾巴

and it has no fur, except on its head
它没有皮毛,除了头上

It still keeps on growing, which is very interesting
它仍然在不断增长,这非常有趣

bears get their growth earlier than this
空头比这更早成长

Bears are dangerous since our catastrophe
自从我们的灾难以来,熊是危险的

soon it will have to have a muzzle on
很快它将不得不戴上枪口

otherwise I won't feel safe around it
否则我不会在它周围感到安全

I have offered to get her a kangaroo if she would let this one go
我提出给她买一只袋鼠,如果她愿意放过这只袋鼠

but she did not appreciate my offer
但她不欣赏我的提议

she is determined to run us into all sorts of foolish risks
她决心让我们冒各种愚蠢的风险

she was not like this before she lost her mind
在她失去理智之前,她不是这样的

A Fortnight Later
两周后

I examined its mouth
我检查了它的嘴巴
There is no danger yet; it has only one tooth
还没有危险;它只有一颗牙齿
It has no tail yet
它还没有尾巴
It makes more noise now than it ever did before
它现在比以往任何时候都发出更多的噪音
and it makes the noise mainly at night
它主要在晚上发出噪音
I have moved out
我已经搬出去了
But I shall go over in the mornings to breakfast
但是我会在早上过去吃早餐
then I will see if it has more teeth
那我看看它是否有更多的牙齿
If it gets a mouthful of teeth, it will be time for it to go
如果它长满了牙齿，就该走了
I won't make an exception if it has no tail
如果它没有尾巴，我不会例外
bears do not need tails in order to be dangerous
熊不需要尾巴才能危险

Four Months Later
四个月后

I have been off hunting and fishing a month
我已经离开打猎和钓鱼一个月了
up in the region that she calls Buffalo
在她称之为布法罗的地区
I don't know why she has called it Buffalo
我不知道她为什么叫它布法罗
it could be because there are not any buffaloes there
可能是因为那里没有水牛
the bear has learned to paddle around all by itself
熊学会了自己划来划去
it can walk on its hind legs
它可以用后腿走路
and it says "daddy" and "mummy" to us
它对我们说"爸爸"和"妈妈"
It is certainly a new species
它当然是一个新物种
This resemblance to words may be purely accidental, of course
当然，这种与单词的相似可能纯粹是偶然的
it may be that its words have no purpose or meaning
可能是它的话没有目的或意义
but even in that case it would still be extraordinary
但即使那样，它仍然是非同寻常的
using words is something which no other bear can do
使用文字是其他熊无法做到的事情
This imitation of speech sufficiently indicates that this is a new kind of bear
这种对言语的模仿足以表明这是一种新型的熊
add to that the general absence of fur
除此之外，一般没有毛皮
and consider the entire absence of a tail
并考虑完全没有尾巴
further study of it will be exceedingly interesting
对它的进一步研究将非常有趣
Meantime I will go off on a far expedition among the forests

of the North
与此同时，我将在北方的森林中进行一次遥远的探险
there I will make a more exhaustive search
在那里我将进行更详尽的搜索
There must certainly be another one somewhere
肯定在某个地方还有另一个
this one will be less dangerous when it has company of its own species
当它有自己物种的公司时，这个危险会更小
I will go straightway
我会直走
but I will muzzle this one first
但我会先封住这个

Three Months Later
三个月后

It has been a weary, weary hunt
这是一场疲惫不堪的狩猎
yet I have had no success
然而我没有成功
while I was gone she caught another one!
当我离开时，她又抓到了一只！
and she didn't even leave the estate
她甚至没有离开庄园
I never saw such luck
我从未见过这样的运气
I might have hunted these woods a hundred years without finding one
我可能已经猎杀了这些树林一百年而没有找到

Next Day - 翌
I have been comparing the new one with the old one
我一直在比较新的和旧的
it is perfectly plain that they are the same breed
很明显，它们是同一品种
I was going to stuff one of them for my collection
我打算为我的收藏塞进其中一个

but she is prejudiced against it for some reason
但她出于某种原因对此有偏见
so I have relinquished the idea
所以我放弃了这个想法
but I think it is a mistake
但我认为这是一个错误
It would be an irreparable loss to science if they should get away
如果他们逃脱,这将是科学无法弥补的损失
The old one is tamer than it was
旧的比以前更温顺
now it can laugh and talk like the parrot
现在它可以像鹦鹉一样大笑和说话
I have no doubt that it has learned this from the parrot
我毫不怀疑它是从鹦鹉那里学到的
I calculate it has a great amount of the imitative faculty
我计算它有大量的模仿能力
I shall be astonished if it turns out to be a new kind of parrot
如果它被证明是一种新型的鹦鹉,我会感到惊讶
and yet I ought not to be astonished
然而我不应该感到惊讶
because it has already been everything else it could think of
因为它已经是它能想到的其他一切
The new one is as ugly now as the old one was at first
新的现在和旧的一样丑陋
it has the same sulphur complexion
它具有相同的硫磺肤色
and it has the same singular head without any fur on it
它有相同的单一头部,上面没有任何毛皮
She calls the new one Abel
她称新的为亚伯

Ten Years Later
十年后

They are boys; we found it out long ago
他们是男孩;我们很久以前就发现了
It was their coming in that small, immature shape that puzzled us
正是它们以那种小而不成熟的形状出现,让我们感到困惑。
we were not used to animals being so small for so long
我们不习惯动物这么小这么久
There are some girls now
现在有一些女孩
Abel is a good boy
亚伯是个好孩子
but if Cain had stayed a bear it would have improved him
但如果该隐保持熊的地位,那会改善他

After all these years I realize I had made a mistake
这么多年过去了,我意识到我犯了一个错误。
I see that I was initially mistaken about Eve
我看到我最初误会了夏娃
it is better to live outside the Garden with her than inside it without her
和她一起住在花园外面总比没有她住在花园里好
At first I thought she talked too much
起初我觉得她话太多了
but now I should be sorry to have that voice fall silent
但现在我应该为那个声音沉默而感到遗憾

I wouldn't want that voice to pass out of my life
我不希望那个声音从我的生命中消失
Blessed be the chestnut that brought us together
让我们走到一起的栗子有福了
this chestnut has taught me to know the goodness of her heart
这栗子教会了我知道她心中的善良
this chestnut has taught me the sweetness of her spirit!
这个栗子教会了我她精神的甜蜜!

- Eve's Diary -
- 夏娃日记 -

Translated from the original, by Mark Twain
翻译自马克吐温的原文

SATURDAY - 星期六
I am almost a whole day old, now
我快一整天了,现在
I arrived yesterday
我昨天到达
That is as it seems to me
在我看来就是这样
And it must be so
一定是这样

perhaps there was a day-before-yesterday
也许有前天
but I was not there when it happened
但当它发生时我不在那里
if I had been there I would remember it
如果我在那里，我会记得它
It could be, of course, that it did happen
当然，它可能确实发生了
and it could be that I was not noticing
可能是我没有注意到
Very well; I will be very watchful now
很好;我现在会非常警惕
if a day-before-yesterday happen I will make a note
如果前天发生，我会做笔记
It will be best to start right
最好从右开始
and it's best not to let the record get confused
最好不要让记录混淆
I feel these details are going to be important
我觉得这些细节会很重要
my instincts are telling me this
我的直觉告诉我这一点
they might be important to historians some day
它们有一天可能对历史学家很重要
For I feel like an experiment
因为我觉得自己像一个实验
I feel exactly like an experiment
我感觉就像一个实验
a person can't feel more like an experiment than I do
一个人不能比我更像一个实验
it would be impossible to feel more like an experiment
感觉更像一个实验是不可能的
and so I am coming to feel convinced that is what I am
所以我开始确信这就是我
I am an experiment
我是一个实验

just an experiment and nothing more
只是一个实验,仅此而已

Then, if I am an experiment, am I the whole of it?
那么,如果我是一个实验,我是它的全部吗?
No, I think I am not the whole experiment
不,我想我不是整个实验
I think the rest of it is part of the experiment too
我认为其余部分也是实验的一部分
I am the main part of the experiment
我是实验的主要部分
but I think the rest of it has its share in the matter
但我认为其余部分在这件事上也有其份额
Is my position in the experiment assured?

我在实验中的位置是否得到保证？
or do I have to watch my position and take care of it?
还是我必须注意我的位置并照顾它？
I think it is the latter, perhaps
我认为是后者，也许
Some instinct tells me guard my role
某种本能告诉我保护自己的角色
eternal vigilance is the price of supremacy
永远的警惕是至高无上的代价
That is a good phrase, I think
我认为这句话很好
it is especially good for someone so young
这对这么年轻的人来说特别好

Everything looks better today than it did yesterday
今天一切看起来都比昨天好

there had been a great rush of finishing up the mountains
完成山脉的匆忙

so things had been left in a ragged condition
所以事情一直处于破烂的状态

and the open plains were so cluttered that
开阔的平原是如此杂乱，以至于

all the aspects and proportions were quite distressing
所有方面和比例都非常令人痛苦

because they still had rubbish and remnants
因为他们还有垃圾和残余物

Noble and beautiful works of art should not be rushed
高贵而美丽的艺术品不应该操之过急

and this majestic new world is indeed a work of art
而这个雄伟的新世界确实是一件艺术品

I can tell it has been made to be noble and beautiful
我看得出来，它已经被塑造成高贵而美丽的

and it is certainly marvellously near to being perfect
它当然非常接近完美

notwithstanding the shortness of the time
尽管时间很短

There are too many stars in some places
有些地方的明星太多了

and there are not enough stars in other places
而且其他地方的星星不够

but that can be remedied soon enough, no doubt
但毫无疑问，这可以很快得到补救

The moon got loose last night and slid down
昨晚月亮松了，滑了下来

it fell out of the scheme
它退出了计划

this was a very great loss
这是一个非常大的损失

it breaks my heart to think of it
想想就心碎

among the ornaments and decorations it is unique

在装饰品和装饰品中，它是独一无二的
nothing is comparable to it for beauty and finish
在美观和光洁度方面没有什么能比得上它
It should have been held in place better
它应该更好地保持到位
I wish we could get it back again
我希望我们能再次拿回它

But there is no telling where it went to
但不知道它去了哪里
And besides, whoever gets it will hide it
此外，谁得到它就会隐藏它
I know it because I would do it myself
我知道，因为我会自己做
I believe I can be honest in all other matters
我相信我可以在所有其他事情上诚实
but I already begin to realize something;
但我已经开始意识到一些事情；
the core of my nature is love of the beautiful
我天性的核心是对美的热爱
I have a passion for the beautiful
我对美丽的充满热情
so it would not be safe to trust me with a moon
所以用月亮托付给我是不安全的
I could give up a moon that I found in the daytime
我可以放弃白天找到的月亮
because I would be afraid someone was looking
因为我害怕有人在看
but if I found a moon in the dark I would keep it
但是如果我在黑暗中找到月亮，我会保留它
I am sure I could find some kind of an excuse
我相信我可以找到某种借口
I would find a way to not say anything about it
我会想办法不说什么
because I do love moons
因为我确实爱月亮
they are so pretty and so romantic
他们是如此美丽，如此浪漫
I wish we had five or six of them
我希望我们有五六个
I would never go to bed
我永远不会上床睡觉
I would never get tired lying on the moss-bank
躺在苔藓岸边我永远不会累
and I would always be looking up at them

我会一直抬头看着他们

Stars are good, too
明星也很好
I wish I could get some to put in my hair
我希望我能得到一些放在我的头发上
But I suppose I can never do that
但我想我永远做不到
it's surprising how far away they are
令人惊讶的是他们有多远
because they do not look like they're far away
因为他们看起来并不遥远
they first showed themselves last night

他们昨晚第一次露面
I tried to knock some down with a pole
我试图用杆子把一些撞倒
but it didn't reach, which astonished me;
但它没有到达,这让我感到惊讶;
then I tried throwing clods at them
然后我试着向他们扔土块
I tried this till I was all tired out
我试过这个,直到我都累了
but I never managed to get one
但我从来没有设法得到一个
It must be because I am left-handed
一定是因为我是左撇子
because of this I cannot throw good
正因为如此,我不能扔好东西
though I did make some close shots
虽然我确实做了一些近距离拍摄
I saw the black blot of the clod
我看到了土块的黑色污点
it sailed right into the midst of the golden clusters
它直接驶入了金色的星团中间
I must have tried forty or fifty times
我一定试过四五十次
and I just barely missed them
我只是几乎没有错过他们
perhaps I should have held out a little longer
也许我应该再坚持一会儿
and then I might have got one
然后我可能会得到一个

So I cried a little, which was natural
所以我哭了一下，这是很自然的
I suppose it is natural for one of my age
我想这对我这个年龄的人来说是很自然的
and after I was rested I got a basket
休息后，我得到了一个篮子
I went to a hill on the extreme rim of the circle
我去了圆圈最边缘的一座小山
there the stars should be closer to the ground
那里的星星应该离地面更近
perhaps if I was there I could get them
也许如果我在那里，我可以得到他们
then I could get them with my hands

然后我可以用手得到它们
this would be better anyway
无论如何这会更好
because then I could gather them tenderly
因为那样我就可以温柔地收集它们
and I would not break them
我不会破坏它们
But it was farther than I thought
但它比我想象的要远
and at last I had to give it up
最后我不得不放弃它
I was so tired from all my trying
我所有的尝试都太累了
I couldn't drag my feet another step
我不能再拖后腿了
and besides, my feet were sore
此外，我的脚很痛
and my feet hurt me very much
我的脚很疼
I couldn't get back home
我回不了家
it was late, and turning cold
天色已晚，天气变冷
but I found some tigers
但我发现了一些老虎
and I nestled in among them
我依偎在他们中间
and it was most adorably comfortable
而且最可爱舒适
and their breath was sweet and pleasant
他们的呼吸甜美宜人
because they live on a diet of strawberries
因为他们以草莓为食
I had never seen a tiger before
我以前从未见过老虎
but I knew straight away by their stripes
但我马上就知道他们的条纹

If only I could have one of those skins
如果我能拥有其中一张皮肤就好了
it would make a lovely gown
它会做一件可爱的礼服

Today I am getting better ideas about distances
今天我对距离有了更好的了解
I was so eager to get hold of every pretty thing
我非常渴望抓住每一个漂亮的东西
I was so eager that I giddily grabbed for it
我太渴望了,我傻乎乎地抓住了它
sometimes I grabbed for it when it was too far away
有时我抓住它太远了

and I grabbed for it when it was but six inches away
当它只有六英寸远时，我抓住了它
I even grabbed for it when it was between thorns!
我什至在荆棘之间抓住了它！
I learned a lesson and I made an axiom
我吸取了教训，我做了一个公理
I made it all out of my own head
我自己做了这一切
it is my very first one
这是我的第一个
THE SCRATCHED EXPERIMENT SHUNS THE THORN
划伤实验避开荆棘
I think it is a very good axiom for one so young
我认为对于一个如此年轻的人来说，这是一个很好的公理

last afternoon I followed the other experiment around
昨天下午我跟着另一个实验
I kept a distance, to see what it might be for
我保持距离，看看它可能是为了什么
But I was not able to establish its use
但我无法确定它的用途
I think it is a man
我认为这是一个男人
I had never seen a man
我从来没见过男人
but it looked like a man
但它看起来像一个男人
and I feel sure that that is what it is
我确信这就是它
I realized something strange about this man
我意识到这个人有些奇怪
I feel more curiosity about it than the other reptiles
我比其他爬行动物对它更有好奇心
I'm assuming it is a reptile
我假设它是一种爬行动物
because it has frowzy hair and blue eyes
因为它有皱眉的头发和蓝色的眼睛

and it looks like a reptile
它看起来像爬行动物
It has no hips and tapers like a carrot when it stands
它没有臀部，站立时像胡萝卜一样变细
it spreads itself apart like a derrick
它像井架一样散开
so I think it is a reptile
所以我认为它是一种爬行动物
although it may be architecture
虽然可能是建筑

I was afraid of it at first
一开始我很害怕

and I started to run every time it turned around
每次它转身我就开始跑
because I thought it was going to chase me
因为我认为它会追我
but by and by I found it was only trying to get away
但渐渐地我发现它只是想逃跑
so after that I was not timid any more
所以在那之后我不再胆怯了
but I tracked behind it by about twenty yards
但我跟在它后面大约二十码
I tracked it for several hours
我跟踪了几个小时
this made it nervous and unhappy
这让它感到紧张和不高兴
At last it was a good deal worried, and climbed a tree
终于很担心了,爬上了一棵树。
I waited a good while
我等了好一会儿
then gave it up and went home
然后放弃了,回家了

SUNDAY - 星期日

Today the same thing happened
今天发生了同样的事情
I got it up the tree again
我又把它弄上了树
It is still up there
它仍然在那里
and it is resting, apparently
显然,它正在休息
But that is a subterfuge
但这是一种诡计
Sunday isn't the day of rest
星期天不是休息的日子
Saturday is appointed for that
星期六被指定为此
It looks to me like a strange creature
在我看来,它就像一个奇怪的生物
it is more interested in resting than in anything else
它对休息比其他任何事情都更感兴趣
It would tire me to rest so much
休息这么多会让我很累
It tires me just to sit around and watch the tree
只是坐着看树就累了
I do wonder what it is for
我确实想知道它是干什么用的
I never see it do anything
我从来没有看到它做任何事情

They returned the moon last night
他们昨晚还了月亮
and I was SO happy!
我太高兴了!
I think it is very honest of them
我认为他们非常诚实
It slid down and fell off again
它滑下来又掉了下来
but I was not distressed
但我并不苦恼
there is no need to worry
无需担心
when one has such kind neighbours, they will fetch it back

当一个人有这么善良的邻居时，他们会把它拿回来
I wish I could do something to show my appreciation
我希望我能做点什么来表达我的感激之情
I would like to send them some stars
我想送他们一些星星
because we have more than we can use
因为我们拥有的比我们能用的多
I do mean to say I, not we
我的意思是说我，而不是我们
I can see that the reptile cares nothing for such things
我可以看到爬行动物对这些事情毫不在乎
It has low tastes and it is not kind
它的品味低，而且不友善
I went there yesterday evening
我昨天晚上去了那里
in the evening it had crept down
傍晚时分，它悄悄地下来了。
and it was trying to catch the little speckled fishes
它试图捕捉小斑点鱼
the little fishes that play in the pool
在游泳池里玩耍的小鱼
and I had to clod it
我不得不把它弄脏
in order to make it go up the tree again
为了让它再次上树
and then it left them alone
然后它让他们一个人呆着
I wonder if that is what it is for?
我想知道这是否是它的用途？
Hasn't it any heart?
难道没有心吗？
Hasn't it any compassion for the little creature?
难道对这个小家伙一点同情心都没有吗？
was it designed and manufactured for such ungentle work?
它是为这种不温柔的工作而设计和制造的吗？
It has the look of being made for silly things
它看起来像是为愚蠢的事情而生的

One of the clods hit the back of its ear
其中一个土块击中了它的耳朵后部
and it used language, which gave me a thrill
它使用了语言，这给了我一种刺激
for it was the first time I had ever heard speech
因为这是我第一次听到演讲
it was the first speech I heard except my own
这是我听到的第一个演讲，除了我自己的演讲
I did not understand the words
我不明白这些话
but the words seemed expressive
但这些话似乎很有表现力

When I found it could talk I felt a new interest in it
当我发现它可以说话时，我对它产生了新的兴趣。
because I love to talk more than anything
因为我喜欢说话胜过一切
I like to talk all day
我喜欢整天聊天
and in my sleep I talk too
在睡梦中我也说话
and I am very interesting
而且我很有趣
but if I had another to talk to I could be twice as interesting
但是如果我有另一个人可以交谈，我可以加倍有趣
and I would never stop talking
我永远不会停止说话

If this reptile is a man, it isn't an it, is it?
如果这只爬行动物是人,它就不是它,是吗?
That wouldn't be grammatical, would it?
那不会是语法上的,对吧?
I think it would be he
我想会是他
In that case one would parse it thus:
在这种情况下,可以这样解析它:
nominative; he
主格;他
dative; him
与格;他
possessive; his
占有;他
Well, I will consider it a man
好吧,我会认为它是一个男人
and I will call it he until it turns out to be something else
我会称它为他,直到事实证明是别的东西
This will be handier than having so many uncertainties
这将比拥有如此多的不确定性更方便。

NEXT WEEK SUNDAY
下周 周日

All the week I tagged around after him
整个星期我都在追着他
and I tried to get acquainted with him
我试图结识他
I had to do the talking because he was shy
我不得不说话，因为他很害羞
but I didn't mind talking
但我不介意说话
He seemed pleased to have me around
他似乎很高兴有我在身边
and I used the sociable 'we' a good deal
我很好地使用了社交的"我们"
because it seemed to flatter him to be included
因为被包括在内似乎很恭维他

WEDNESDAY - 星期三
We are getting along very well now
我们现在相处得很好
and we're getting better and better acquainted
我们越来越熟悉
He does not try to avoid me any more, which is a good sign
他不再试图避开我,这是一个好兆头
and it shows that he likes to have me with him, which pleases me
这表明他喜欢和我在一起,这让我高兴
and I study to be useful to him
我学习是为了对他有用
I want to be useful in every way I can
我想尽我所能成为有用的人
so as to increase his regard of me
以增加他对我的重视

During the last day or two - 在最后一两天
I have taken all the work of naming things off his hands
我已经把所有命名事情的工作从他手中拿走了
and this has been a great relief to him
这对他来说是一个很大的安慰。
for he has no gift in that line of work
因为他在那一行没有天赋
and he is evidently very grateful
他显然非常感激
He can't think of a rational name to save himself
他想不出一个合理的名字来拯救自己
but I do not let him see that I am aware of his defect
但我不让他看到我知道他的缺陷
Whenever a new creature comes along I name it
每当有新生物出现时,我都会给它命名
before he has time to expose himself by an awkward silence
还没来得及用尴尬的沉默暴露自己
In this way I have saved him many embarrassments
这样我就省去了他很多尴尬
I have no defect like this
我没有这样的缺陷
The minute I set eyes on an animal I know what it is
当我看到一只动物的那一刻,我就知道它是什么了。
I don't have to reflect even for a moment
我甚至不必反思片刻
the right name comes out instantly
正确的名字立即出现
just as if it were an inspiration
仿佛是一种灵感
I have no doubt it is
我毫不怀疑这是
because I am sure it wasn't in me half a minute before
因为我确定半分钟前它不在我身上
I seem to know just by the shape of the creature
我似乎只知道生物的形状
and I know the way it acts what animal it is
我从它的行为方式知道它是什么动物

When the dodo came along he thought it was a wildcat
当渡渡鸟出现时,他以为是一只野猫。
I saw it in his eyes
我从他的眼睛里看到了
But I saved him from embarrassment
但我把他从尴尬中救了出来
I was careful not to do it in a way that could hurt his pride
我小心翼翼地不以可能伤害他自尊的方式这样做。
I just spoke up as if pleasantly surprised
我只是说出来,好像很惊喜
I didn't speak as if I was dreaming of conveying information
我没有说话,好像我梦想传达信息
"Well, I do declare, if there isn't the dodo!"

"好吧,如果没有渡渡鸟,我宣布!"
I explained without seeming to be explaining
我解释时似乎没有解释
I explained how I knew it was a dodo
我解释了我是如何知道这是渡渡鸟的
I thought maybe he was a little piqued
我想也许他有点生气
I knew the creature when he didn't
我认识这个生物,而他不知道
but it was quite evident that he admired me
但很明显,他很欣赏我
That was very agreeable
这是非常令人满意的
and I thought of it more than once with gratification before I slept
我不止一次在睡觉前心满意足地想到它
How little a thing can make us happy
一件多么小的事情能让我们快乐
we're happy when we feel that we have earned it!
当我们觉得自己赚到了它时,我们会很高兴!

THURSDAY - 星期四

my first sorrow
我的第一个悲伤

Yesterday he avoided me
昨天他避开了我

and he seemed to wish I would not talk to him
他似乎希望我不要和他说话

I could not believe it
我简直不敢相信

and I thought there was some mistake
我以为有些错误

because I loved to be with him
因为我喜欢和他在一起

and loved to hear him talk
喜欢听他说话

and so how could it be that he could feel unkind toward me?
所以他怎么会对我不友善呢？

I had not done anything wrong
我没有做错任何事

But it seemed true, so I went away
但这似乎是真的，所以我走了

and I sat lonely in the place where I first saw him
我孤独地坐在我第一次见到他的地方

on the morning that we were made
在我们被制造的那天早上

when I did not know what he was
当我不知道他是什么时

when I was still indifferent about him
当我还对他无动于衷时

but now it was a mournful place
但现在这是一个悲伤的地方

and every little thing spoke of him
每一件小事都谈到了他

and my heart was very sore
我的心很痛

I did not really know why I was feeling like this

我真的不知道我为什么会有这种感觉
because it was a new feeling
因为这是一种新的感觉
I had not experienced it before
我以前没有经历过
and it was all a mystery to me
这对我来说都是一个谜
and I could not make sense of it
我无法理解它

But when night came I could not bear the lonesomeness
但当夜幕降临时,我无法忍受寂寞
I went to the new shelter which he had built
我去了他建造的新避难所
I went to ask him what I had done that was wrong
我去问他我做错了什么
and I wanted to know how I could mend it
我想知道我该如何修补它
I wanted to get back his kindness again
我想再次找回他的好意
but he put me out in the rain
但他把我放在雨中
and it was my first sorrow
这是我的第一个悲伤

SUNDAY - 星期日
It is pleasant again and now I am happy
又是愉快的，现在我很开心
but those were heavy days
但那是沉重的日子
I do not think of those days when I can help it
我想不到那些我能帮助它的日子

I tried to get him some of those apples
我试着给他买一些苹果。
but I cannot learn to throw straight
但我不能学会直接投掷
I failed, but I think the good intention pleased him
我失败了,但我认为善意让他高兴
They are forbidden
他们是被禁止的
and he says I would come to harm if I ate one
他说如果我吃了一个我会受到伤害
but then I would come to harm through pleasing him
但后来我会通过取悦他来伤害他
why should I care for that harm?
我为什么要关心这种伤害?

MONDAY
星期一
This morning I told him my name
今天早上我告诉他我的名字
I hoped it would interest him
我希望他会感兴趣
But he did not care for it, which is strange
但他不在乎,这很奇怪
If he should tell me his name I would care
如果他告诉我他的名字,我会在乎
I think it would be pleasanter in my ears than any other sound
我认为它在我的耳朵里会比任何其他声音都更悦耳

He talks very little
他话很少
Perhaps it is because he is not bright
也许是因为他不聪明
and maybe he is sensitive about his intellect
也许他对自己的智力很敏感
it could be that he wishes to conceal it
可能是他想隐瞒
It is such a pity that he should feel this way
太可惜了,他竟然有这种感觉
because intelligence is nothing
因为智能什么都不是
it is in the heart that the values lie

价值观在心中
I wish I could make him understand
我希望我能让他明白
a loving good heart is riches
一颗充满爱心的善良的心是财富
intellect without a good heart is poverty
没有善良的心的智力是贫穷
Although he talks so little, he has quite a considerable vocabulary
虽然他话很少，但他的词汇量相当可观
This morning he used a surprisingly good word
今天早上他用了一个令人惊讶的好词
He evidently recognized that it was a good one
他显然认识到这是一个好人。
because he made sure to use the word a couple more times
因为他确保多用几次这个词
it showed that he possesses a certain quality of perception
这表明他拥有一定的感知能力
Without a doubt that seed can be made to grow, if cultivated
毫无疑问，如果栽培，种子可以生长
Where did he get that word?
他从哪里得到这个词？
I do not think I have ever used that word
我想我从来没有用过这个词
No, he took no interest in my name
不，他对我的名字不感兴趣
I tried to hide my disappointment
我试图掩饰我的失望
but I suppose I did not succeed
但我想我没有成功

I went away and sat on the moss-bank
我走开了,坐在苔藓岸上
and I put my feet into the water
我把脚伸进水里
It is where I go when I hunger for companionship
当我渴望陪伴时,这就是我去的地方
when I want someone to look at
当我想让别人看
when I want someone to talk to
当我想找人说话时
the lovely white body painted in the pool is not enough
游泳池里画的可爱的白色身体是不够的
but it is something, at least

但它是一些东西，至少
and something is better than utter loneliness
有些事情总比完全的孤独要好
It talks when I talk
当我说话时它会说话
it is sad when I am sad
难过的时候就难过
it comforts me with its sympathy
它用它的同情安慰我
it says, "Do not be downhearted, you poor friendless girl"
它说："不要灰心，你这个可怜的没有朋友的女孩"
"I will be your friend"
"我会成为你的朋友"
It is a good friend to me
它是我的好朋友
it is my only friend and my sister
这是我唯一的朋友和妹妹

I shall never forget first time she forsook me!
我永远不会忘记她第一次抛弃我！
My heart was heavy in my body!
我的心在身体里很沉重！
I said, "She was all I had"
我说："她就是我的全部"
"and now she is gone!"
"现在她走了！"
In my despair I said "Break, my heart"
在绝望中，我说"破碎，我的心"
"I cannot bear my life any more!"
"我不能再忍受我的生活了！"
and I hid my face in my hands
我把脸藏在手里
and there was no solace for me
对我来说没有安慰
And when I took my hands away from my face
当我把手从脸上移开时
and after a little, there she was again
过了一会儿，她又来了
white and shining and beautiful
白皙闪亮美丽
and I sprang into her arms
我扑进她的怀里

That was perfect happiness
那是完美的幸福
I had known happiness before, but it was not like this
我以前知道幸福，但不是这样的
this happiness was ecstasy
这种幸福是狂喜
I never doubted her afterwards
事后我再也没有怀疑过她
Sometimes she stayed away for perhaps an hour
有时她会离开一个小时
maybe she was gone almost the whole day
也许她几乎一整天都不见了
but I waited and I did not doubt her return
但我等了，我不怀疑她的回归
I said, "She is busy" or "she is gone on a journey"
我说，"她很忙"或"她去旅行了"
but I know she will come back, and she always did
但我知道她会回来的，而且她一直这样做
At night she would not come if it was dark
晚上天黑了她就不来了
because she was a timid little thing
因为她是个胆小的小东西
but if there was a moon she would come
但如果有月亮，她会来的
I am not afraid of the dark
我不怕黑
but she is younger than I am
但她比我年轻
she was born after I was
她是在我出生之后
Many and many are the visits I have paid her
很多很多都是我拜访过她
she is my comfort and refuge when my life is hard
当我的生活艰难时，她是我的安慰和避难所
and my life is mainly made from hard moments
而我的生活主要是由艰难的时刻组成的

TUESDAY - 星期二

All the morning I was at work improving the estate
整个早上我都在工作，改善庄园
and I purposely kept away from him
我故意远离他
in the hope that he would get lonely and come
希望他会寂寞而来
But he did not come to me
但他没有来找我
At noon I stopped for the day
中午我停了一天
and I took my recreation
我采取了我的娱乐活动
I flitted about with the bees and the butterflies
我和蜜蜂和蝴蝶一起飞来飞去
and I revelled in the flowers
我陶醉在花朵中
those beautiful happy little creatures
那些美丽快乐的小生物
they catch the smile of God out of the sky
他们从天空中捕捉到上帝的微笑
and they preserve the smile!
他们保留了微笑！
I gathered them and made them into wreaths
我把它们收集起来，做成花圈
and I clothed myself in flowers
我给自己披上了花
I ate my luncheon; apples
我吃了午饭;苹果
of course; then I sat in the shade
答案是肯定的;然后我坐在阴凉处
and I wished and waited
我希望并等待
But he did not come
但他没有来

But it is of no loss
但这并不损失
Nothing would have come of it
什么都不会发生
because he does not care for flowers
因为他不在乎花
He called them rubbish
他称它们为垃圾
and he cannot tell one from another
他分不清彼此
and he thinks it is superior to feel like that
他认为有这样的感觉是优越的
He does not care for me, flowers

他不在乎我，花
nor does he care for the painted sky in the evening
他也不在乎晚上的彩绘天空
is there anything he does care for?
他有什么在乎的吗？
he cares for nothing except building shacks
除了建造棚屋，他什么都不在乎
he builds them to coop himself up
他建造它们来笼养自己
but he's away from the good clean rain
但他远离了干净的雨
and he does not sample the fruits
而且他不品尝水果

I laid a dry stick on the ground
我把一根干棍子放在地上
and I tried to bore a hole in it with another one
我试图用另一个在上面钻一个洞
in order to carry out a scheme that I had
为了执行我拥有的计划
and soon I got an awful fright
很快我就吓坏了
A thin, transparent bluish film rose out of the hole
一层薄薄的透明蓝色薄膜从洞中升起
and I dropped everything and ran
我放下一切跑了
I thought it was a spirit
我以为是精神
and I was so frightened!
我太害怕了！
But I looked back and it was not coming;
但我回头一看，它并没有到来；
so I leaned against a rock
所以我靠在一块石头上
and I rested and panted
我休息和喘气
and I let my limbs go on trembling
我让我的四肢继续颤抖
finally they were steady again
终于他们又稳定了
then I crept warily back
然后我小心翼翼地蹑手蹑脚地回来
I was alert, watching, and ready to fly
我警觉，观察，准备飞行
I would run if there was occasion
如果有机会，我会跑
when I was near I parted the branches of a rose-bush
当我靠近时，我分开了玫瑰丛的树枝
and I peeped through the rose-bush
我透过玫瑰丛
and I wished the man was about

我希望那个人是关于
I was looking so cunning and pretty
我看起来很狡猾，很漂亮
but the spirit was gone
但是精神消失了
I went where the spirit was
我去了精神所在的地方
there was a pinch of delicate pink dust in the hole
洞里有一撮精致的粉红色灰尘
I put my finger in to feel it
我把手指伸进去感受它
and I said "ouch!"
我说："哎哟！
and I took it out again
我又把它拿出来了
It was a cruel pain
这是一种残酷的痛苦
I put my finger in my mouth
我把手指放进嘴里
I stood on one foot and then the other, grunting
我一只脚站着，然后另一只脚站着，咕噜咕噜地叫着
I presently eased my misery
我暂时缓解了我的痛苦
then I was full of interest and I began to examine
然后我就饶有兴趣了，我开始检查

I was curious to know what the pink dust was
我很想知道粉红色的灰尘是什么
Suddenly the name of it occurred to me
突然我想到了它的名字
I had never heard of it before
我以前从未听说过
but I knew it was FIRE!
但我知道那是火!
I was as certain of it
我同样确定
as certain as a person could be of anything in the world
就像一个人可以是世界上的任何东西一样确定
So without hesitation I named it that — fire
所以我毫不犹豫地把它命名为——火。

I had created something that didn't exist before
我创造了以前不存在的东西
I had added a new thing to the world
我为世界增添了新事物
this world full of uncountable phenomena
这个充满无数现象的世界
I realized this and I was proud of my achievement
我意识到了这一点，我为我的成就感到自豪
and was going to run and find him
并打算跑去找他
I wanted tell him about it
我想告诉他这件事
I thought it might raise myself in his esteem

我想这可能会提高自己的尊敬
but I reflected on it
但我反思了一下
and I did not do it
我没有这样做
No, he would not care for it
不，他不会在乎的
He would ask what it was good for
他会问它有什么好处
and what could I answer?
我能回答什么？
it was not good for something, it was merely beautiful
它对某事没有好处，它只是美丽

So I sighed, and I did not go
于是我叹了口气，没有去
Because it wasn't good for anything
因为它对任何事情都没有好处
it could not build a shack
它无法建造棚屋
it could not improve melon
它不能改善甜瓜
it could not hurry a fruit crop
它不能赶水果作物
it was useless and foolish vanity
这是无用和愚蠢的虚荣心
he would despise it and say cutting words
他会鄙视它，说切入的话语
But to me it was not despicable
但对我来说，这并不卑鄙
I said, "Oh, you fire, I love you"
我说："哦，你火，我爱你"
"you dainty pink creature, you are BEAUTIFUL"
"你这个精致的粉红色生物，你很漂亮"
"and being beautiful is enough!"
"漂亮就够了！"
and I was going to gather it to my breast, but refrained
我打算把它收集到我的乳房上，但克制住了
Then I thought of another maxim
然后我想到了另一句格言
it was very similar to the first one
它与第一个非常相似
I was afraid it was a plagiarism
我怕是抄袭
"THE BURNT EXPERIMENT SHUNS THE FIRE"
"燃烧的实验避免了火灾"
I repeated my experiment
我重复了我的实验
I had made a good deal of fire-dust
我制造了很多火尘
and I emptied it into a handful of dry brown grass

我把它倒空到一把干棕色的草中
I was intending to carry it home
我打算把它带回家
and I wanted to keep it and play with it
我想保留它并玩它
but the wind struck it and it sprayed up
但是风打了它,它喷了起来
and it spat out at me fiercely
它狠狠地向我吐了口唾沫
and I dropped it and ran
我放下它跑了
When I looked back the blue spirit was towering up
当我回头看时,蓝色的精灵正在耸立
and it was stretching and rolling away like a cloud
它像云一样伸展和滚动
and instantly I thought of the name of it — SMOKE!
我立刻想到了它的名字——烟!
and upon my word, I had never heard of smoke before
根据我的话,我以前从未听说过烟

Soon brilliant yellow and red flares shot up
很快,灿烂的黄色和红色耀斑射了出来。
they shot up through the smoke
他们在烟雾中冲了上来
and I named them in an instant — FLAMES
我瞬间给它们起了名字——火焰
and I was right about this too
而且在这一点上也是对的
even though these were the very first flames there had ever been
尽管这是有史以来的第一场火焰
They climbed the trees and they flashed splendidly
他们爬上树,闪闪发光
there was increasing volume of tumbling smoke
翻滚的烟雾越来越多
and the flames danced in and out of the smoke
火焰在烟雾中跳进跳出
and I had to clap my hands and laugh and dance
我不得不拍手,笑着跳舞
it was so new and strange
太新奇了,太奇怪了
and it was so wonderful and beautiful!
它是如此美妙和美丽!

He came running, and he stopped and gazed
他跑了过来，他停了下来，凝视着
he said not a word for many minutes
他好几分钟一言不发
Then he asked what it was
然后他问这是什么
it a shame he asked such a direct question
可惜他问了这么直接的问题
I had to answer it, of course, and I did
当然，我必须回答它，我做到了
if it annoyed him, what could I do?
如果惹恼了他，我该怎么办？
it's not my fault that I knew what it was
我知道那是什么不是我的错
I said it was fire
我说是火
I had no desire to annoy him
我不想惹恼他
After a pause he asked: "How did it come?"
顿了顿，他问道："怎么来的？
this question also had to have a direct answer
这个问题也要有直接的答案
"I made it" I answered
"我成功了"我回答
The fire was travelling farther and farther away
火势越走越远
He went to the edge of the burned place
他走到了被烧毁的地方的边缘
and he stood looking down at it
他站在那里低头看着它
and he said: "What are these?"
他说："这些是什么？
I told him they were fire-coals
我告诉他他们是火炭
He picked up one to examine it

他拿起一个检查
but he changed his mind and put it down again
但他改变了主意,又放下了
Then he went away
然后他就走了
NOTHING interests him
没有什么让他感兴趣

But I was interested
但我感兴趣
There were ashes, gray and soft and delicate and pretty
有灰烬,灰蒙蒙的,柔软的,精致的,漂亮的
I knew what they were straight away

我马上就知道他们是什么了
And the embers; I knew the embers, too
还有余烬;我也知道余烬
I found my apples and I raked them out
我找到了我的苹果，我把它们耙了出来
and I was glad because I am very young
我很高兴，因为我很年轻
so my appetite is still very active
所以我的胃口还是很活跃的
But I was disappointed by the experiment
但我对实验感到失望
because all the apples were burst open and spoiled
因为所有的苹果都被爆裂并变质了
at least, I thought they were spoiled
至少，我以为他们被宠坏了
but they were not actually spoiled
但他们实际上并没有被宠坏
they were better than raw ones
他们比生的好
Fire is beautiful and some day it will be useful, I think
火是美丽的，总有一天它会有用，我想

FRIDAY - 星期五

I saw him again, for a moment
我又见到了他，有一会儿
last Monday at nightfall, but only for a moment
上周一夜幕降临时，但只是片刻
I was hoping he would praise me for trying to improve the estate
我希望他会表扬我试图改善庄园
because I had meant well and had worked hard
因为我本意很好，很努力
But he was not pleased and he turned away and left me
但他不高兴，他转身离开了我。
He was also displeased on another account
他对另一个帐户也很不高兴
I tried to persuade him to stop going over the water falls
我试图说服他不要再越过瀑布了。
the fire had revealed to me a new feeling
大火向我揭示了一种新的感觉
this feeling was quite new
这种感觉很新
it felt distinctly different from love or grief
感觉与爱或悲伤截然不同
and it was different from the other passions I had discovered
它与我发现的其他激情不同
this new feeling was FEAR and it is horrible!
这种新感觉是恐惧，太可怕了！
I wish I had never discovered it
我希望我从未发现过它
it gives me dark moments and spoils my happiness
它给了我黑暗的时刻，破坏了我的幸福
it makes me shiver and tremble and shudder
它让我颤抖，颤抖和颤抖
But I could not persuade him
但我无法说服他
he has not discovered fear yet
他还没有发现恐惧

so he could not understand me
所以他听不懂我的话

- Extract from Adam's Diary -
- 摘自亚当日记 -

Perhaps I ought to remember that she is very young
也许我应该记住,她还很年轻。
she is still but a mere girl
她仍然只是一个女孩
and I should make allowances
我应该让
She is all interest, eagerness, vivacity
她都是兴趣,渴望,活泼
she finds the world endlessly charming
她发现世界无穷无尽的魅力
a wonder, a mystery, a joy
一个奇迹,一个谜,一个喜悦

she can't speak for delight when she finds a new flower
当她找到一朵新花时,她无法高兴
she must pet it and caress it
她必须抚摸它并爱抚它
and she has to smell it and talk to it
她必须闻到它并与之交谈
and she pours out endearing names upon it
她倾吐出可爱的名字
And she is color-mad; brown rocks, yellow sand
她是颜色疯狂的;棕色岩石,黄色沙子
gray moss, green foliage, blue sky, the pearl of the dawn
灰色的苔藓,绿色的树叶,蓝天,黎明的珍珠
the purple shadows on the mountains
山上的紫色阴影
the golden islands floating in crimson seas at sunset
日落时漂浮在深红色海洋中的金色岛屿
the pallid moon sailing through the shredded cloud-rack
苍白的月亮在破碎的云架上航行
the star-jewels glittering in the wastes of space
在太空废墟中闪闪发光的星星宝石
none of these names are of any practical value
这些名称都没有任何实用价值
there's no value in them as far as I can see
据我所知,它们没有任何价值
but they have color and majesty
但他们有色彩和威严
and that is enough for her
这对她来说已经足够了
and she loses her mind over them
她对他们失去了理智
If only she could quiet down a little
要是她能安静一点就好了
I wish she kept still a couple minutes at a time
我希望她一次保持几分钟不动
it would be a reposeful spectacle
这将是一个宁静的奇观
In that case I think I could enjoy looking at her

在那种情况下，我想我可以喜欢看着她
indeed, I am sure I could enjoy her company
确实，我相信我可以享受她的陪伴
I am coming to realize that she is a quite remarkable creature
我开始意识到她是一个非常了不起的生物
lithe, slender, trim, rounded
轻盈、纤细、修剪、圆形
shapely, nimble, graceful
匀称、灵活、优雅
and once she was standing as white as marble
有一次她站得像大理石一样白
she was on a boulder, and drenched in the sun
她在一块巨石上，沐浴在阳光下
she stood with her young head tilted back
她站着，年轻的头向后仰着。
and her hand was shading her eyes
她的手遮住了她的眼睛
she was watching the flight of a bird in the sky
她在看天上一只鸟的飞翔
I recognized that she was beautiful
我认出她很漂亮

MONDAY NOON - 周一中午

Is there anything that she is not interested in?
有什么她不感兴趣的吗？
if there is something, it is not in my list
如果有的话，它不在我的列表中
There are animals that I am indifferent to
有些动物我无动于衷
but it is not so with her
但她不是这样
She has no discrimination
她没有歧视
she takes to all the animals
她带走所有的动物
she thinks they are all treasures
她认为它们都是宝藏
every new animal is welcome
欢迎每一种新动物

take the mighty brontosaurus as an example
以强大的暴龙为例
she regarded it as an acquisition
她认为这是一次收购
I considered it a calamity
我认为这是一场灾难
that is a good sample of the lack of harmony
这是缺乏和谐的一个很好的例子
a lack of harmony between our views of things
我们对事物的看法之间缺乏和谐
She wanted to domesticate it
她想驯化它
I wanted to give it the house and move out
我想把房子给它搬出去
She believed it could be tamed by kind treatment
她相信可以通过善意的对待来驯服它
and she thought it would be a good pet
她认为这会是一只好宠物
I tried to convince her otherwise
我试图说服她
a pet twenty-one feet high is no thing to have at home
二十一英尺高的宠物在家里是没有东西的
even with the best intentions it could sit down on the house
即使有最好的意图,它也可以坐在房子上
it wouldn't have to mean any harm
这不一定意味着任何伤害
but it could still mash the house quite easily
但它仍然可以很容易地捣碎房子
for anyone could see that it was absent-minded
因为任何人都能看出这是心不在焉的
because it had an emptiness behind its eyes
因为它的眼睛后面有一种空虚
Still, her heart was set upon having that monster
尽管如此,她的心还是一心想拥有那个怪物。
and she couldn't give it up
她不能放弃
She thought we could start a dairy with it

她认为我们可以用它开一家乳制品
and she wanted me to help milk it
她想让我帮忙挤奶
but I wouldn't milk it
但我不会挤奶
it was too risky
风险太大
The sex wasn't right for milking either
性爱也不适合挤奶
and we didn't have a ladder anyway
反正我们没有梯子
Then she wanted to ride it
然后她想骑它
she thought she would get a better view of the scenery
她以为她会更好地看到风景
Thirty or forty feet of its tail was lying on the ground
它的尾巴有三四十英尺躺在地上
it had all the size of a fallen tree
它有一棵倒下的树那么大
and she thought she could climb it
她以为她可以爬上去
but she was mistaken
但她错了
when she got to the steep place it was too slick
当她到达陡峭的地方时,它太光滑了
and she came sliding back down
她又滑了下来。
she would have hurt herself if it wasn't for me
如果不是我,她会伤害自己

Was she satisfied now? No
她现在满意了吗?不
Nothing ever satisfies her but demonstration
没有什么能满足她,只有示范
she didn't keep theories untested for long
她没有长时间不经测试理论
It is the right spirit, I concede
这是正确的精神,我承认
it is what attracts me to her
这就是吸引我的原因
I feel the influence of it
我感受到了它的影响
if I were with her more I think I would become more adventurous

如果我和她在一起更多，我想我会变得更冒险
Well, she had one theory remaining about this colossus
好吧，她对这个庞然大物还有一个理论
she thought that if we could tame it we could stand in the river
她想，如果我们能驯服它，我们就可以站在河里。
if we made him our friend we could use him as a bridge
如果我们让他成为我们的朋友，我们可以把他当作桥梁。
It turned out that he was already plenty tame enough
事实证明，他已经足够驯服了
he was tame enough as far as she was concerned
就她而言，他已经足够温顺了
so she tried her theory, but it failed
所以她尝试了她的理论，但失败了
she got him properly placed in the river
她把他正确地放在河里
and she went ashore to cross over him
她上岸越过他
but he came out and followed her around
但他出来了，跟着她到处走。
like a pet mountain
像宠物山
Like the other animals
像其他动物一样
They all do that
他们都这样做

- Eve's Diary -
- 夏娃日记 –

Tuesday, Wednesday, Thursday, and today:
周二、周三、周四和今天：
I didn't see him any of these days
这些天我都没见到他
It is a long time to be alone
一个人呆着很久
still, it is better to be alone than unwelcome
不过，独处总比不受欢迎好

FRIDAY - 星期五
I HAD to have company
我必须有陪伴
I was made for having company, I think
我想，我是为了有陪伴而生的
so I made friends with the animals
所以我和动物交了朋友
They are just so charming
他们是如此迷人
and they have the kindest disposition
他们有最善良的性情
and they have the politest ways
他们有最政治的方式
they never look sour or let you feel that you are intruding
他们从不看起来酸涩或让你觉得你在入侵
they smile at you and wag their tail
他们对你微笑并摇尾巴
at least, they wag their tale if they've got one
至少，如果他们有一个，他们会摇摆他们的故事
and they are always ready for a romp or an excursion
他们随时准备嬉戏或短途旅行
they're ready for anything you want to propose
他们已经准备好接受您想提出的任何建议
I think they are perfect gentlemen
我认为他们是完美的绅士
All these days we have had such good times
这些天来，我们度过了如此美好的时光
and it hasn't been lonesome for me, ever
对我来说，从来没有寂寞过

Lonesome? No, I should say not
寂寞？不，我应该说不是
there's always a swarm of them around
周围总是有一群人
sometimes as much as four or five acres
有时多达四五英亩
when you stand on a rock you can see them for miles
当你站在一块岩石上时，你可以看到他们几英里
they are mottled and splashed and gay with color
他们斑驳，飞溅，同性恋与颜色
and there's a frisking sheen and sun-flash
还有闪闪发光的光泽和阳光闪光
and the landscape is so rippled with stripes
风景被条纹涟漪

you might think it was a lake
你可能认为这是一个湖

but you know it isn't a lake at all
但你知道它根本不是一个湖

and there are storms of sociable birds
还有善于交际的鸟类风暴

and there are hurricanes of whirring wings
还有呼啸的翅膀飓风

and the sun strikes all that feathery commotion
太阳打在了所有羽毛般的骚动中

you can see a blazing up of all the colors you can think of
你可以看到你能想到的所有颜色的燃烧

enough colours to put your eyes out
足够的颜色让你的眼睛睁开

We have made long excursions
我们进行了长途旅行
and I have seen a great deal of the world
我见过很多世界
I think I've seen almost all of it
我想我几乎都看过了
I must be first traveler
我必须是第一个旅行者
and I am the only traveller
我是唯一的旅行者
When we are on the march, it is an imposing sight
当我们在行军中时,这是一个壮观的景象
there's nothing like it anywhere
任何地方都没有类似的东西
For comfort I ride a tiger or a leopard
为了舒适,我骑老虎或豹子
because they are soft and have round backs that fit me
因为它们很柔软,有适合我的圆背
and because they are such pretty animals
因为它们是如此漂亮的动物
but for long distance, or for scenery, I ride the elephant
但为了长途,或者为了风景,我骑大象
He hoists me up with his trunk
他用他的行李箱把我吊起来
but I can get off myself
但我可以自己下车
when we are ready to camp he sits
当我们准备露营时,他坐着
and I slide down off his back
我从他的背上滑下来

The birds and animals are all friendly to each other
鸟类和动物彼此友好
and there are no disputes about anything
而且对任何事情都没有争议
They all talk with each other and to me
他们都互相交谈，并与我交谈
but it must be a foreign language
但它必须是一门外语
because I cannot make out a word they say
因为我听不清他们说的一句话
yet they often understand me when I talk back
然而当我顶嘴时，他们经常理解我
the dog and the elephant understand me particularly well
狗和大象特别了解我

It makes me ashamed
这让我感到羞愧
It shows that they are more intelligent than I am
这表明他们比我更聪明
but I want to be the main experiment
但我想成为主要实验
and I intend to be the main experiment
我打算成为主要实验
I have learned a number of things
我学到了很多东西
and I am educated, now
我受过教育,现在
but I wasn't educated at first
但一开始我没有受过教育
I was ignorant at first
起初我很无知
At first it used to vex me
起初它曾经困扰着我
because I was never smart enough
因为我从来都不够聪明
I wasn't smart enough despite how much I observed
尽管我观察了多少,但我不够聪明
I was never around when the water was running uphill
当水流上坡时,我从来没有在身边
but now I do not mind it
但现在我不介意
I have experimented and experimented
我做过实验,又做过实验
I know it never runs uphill, except in the dark
我知道它从不上坡,除非在黑暗中
I know it does run uphill when it is dark
我知道天黑的时候它确实会上坡
because the pool never goes dry
因为游泳池永远不会干涸
it would dry up if the water didn't come back in the night
如果晚上水不回来,它会干涸
It is best to prove things by actual experiment

最好通过实际实验来证明事物
if you do an experiment then you KNOW
如果你做一个实验,那么你就知道
whereas if you depend on guessing you never get educated
而如果你依靠猜测,你永远不会受过教育

thinking about things is not enough either
思考问题也不够
Some things you CAN'T find out
有些事情你找不到
but you will never know you can't by guessing and supposing:
但你永远不会知道你不能通过猜测和假设：
no, you have to be patient and go on experimenting
不，你必须耐心等待并继续尝试
until you find out that you can't find out
直到你发现你找不到
And it is delightful to have it that way
以这种方式拥有它是令人愉快的
it makes the world so interesting
它让世界变得如此有趣
If there wasn't anything to find out, it would be dull
如果没有什么可发现的，那就沉闷了
Even not finding out is just as interesting
即使没有发现也同样有趣
sometimes not finding out is as interesting as finding out
有时不发现和发现一样有趣
The secret of the water was a treasure until I got it
水的秘密是宝藏，直到我得到它
then the excitement all went away
然后兴奋都消失了
and I recognized a sense of loss
我意识到一种失落感

By experiment I know that wood swims
通过实验我知道木头会游泳

dry leaves, feathers, and other things float too
干燥的树叶、羽毛和其他东西也会漂浮

so you can know that a rock can swim
所以你可以知道岩石会游泳

because you've collected cumulative evidence
因为你已经收集了累积的证据

but you have to put up with simply knowing it
但你必须忍受简单地知道它

because there isn't any way to prove it
因为没有任何办法证明它

at least up until now there's no way to prove it

至少到目前为止,没有办法证明这一点
But I shall find a way
但我会找到办法的
then that excitement will go
然后那种兴奋就会消失
Such things make me sad
这样的事情让我很难过
by and by I will come to know everything
渐渐地,我会知道一切
and then there won't be any more excitement
然后就不会再有兴奋了
and I do love excitements so much!
我非常喜欢刺激!
The other night I couldn't sleep
那天晚上我睡不着
I was thinking so much about it
我想了很多

At first I couldn't establish what I was made for
起初我无法确定我是为了什么而生的
but now I think I know what I was made for
但现在我想我知道我是为了什么而生的
I was made to search out the secrets of this wonderful world
我被迫寻找这个美好世界的秘密
and I am made to be happy
我生来就是快乐的
I think the Giver of it all for devising it
我认为这一切的给予者是为了设计它
I think there are still many things to learn
我认为还有很多东西需要学习
and I hope there will always be more to learn
我希望总会有更多的东西要学
by not hurrying too fast I think they will last weeks and weeks
通过不要太快，我认为他们会持续数周和数周
I hope I have so much left to discover
我希望我还有很多东西要发现
When you cast up a feather it sails away on the air
当你抛出一根羽毛时，它会在空中扬帆远去
and then it goes out of sight
然后它就消失了
when you throw up a clod it doesn't act like a feather
当你扔出一块土块时，它不会像羽毛一样
It comes down, every time
每次都下来
I have tried it and tried it
我试过了，试过了
and it is always this way
而且总是这样
I wonder why it is
我想知道为什么会这样
Of course it DOESN'T come down
当然不会下来
but why does it SEEM to come down?
但为什么它似乎下降了？

I suppose it is an optical illusion
我想这是一种视错觉

I mean, one of them is an optical illusion
我的意思是,其中之一是视错觉

I don't know which one is an optical illusion
我不知道哪一个是视错觉

It may be the feather, it may be the clod
可能是羽毛,可能是土块

I can't prove which it is
我无法证明它是哪个

I can only demonstrate that one or the other is a fake
我只能证明一个或另一个是假的

and I let you take your choice
我让你选择你

By watching, I know that the stars are not going to last
通过观看,我知道星星不会持续下去
I have seen some of the best ones melt
我见过一些最好的融化
and then they ran down the sky
然后他们跑下天空
Since one can melt, they can all melt
既然一个人可以融化,他们都可以融化
since they can all melt, they can all melt the same night
既然它们都可以融化,所以它们都可以在同一天晚上融化
That sorrow will come, I know it
悲伤会来的,我知道
I mean to sit up every night and look at them
我的意思是每天晚上坐起来看看他们
as long as I can keep awake
只要我能保持清醒
and I will impress those sparkling fields on my memory
我会在我的记忆中留下那些闪闪发光的田野
so that I can by my fancy restore those lovely myriads
这样我就可以按照我的幻想恢复那些可爱的无数
then I can put them back into the black sky, when they are taken away
然后我可以把它们放回黑天,当它们被带走时
and I can make them sparkle again
我可以让他们再次闪闪发光
and I can double them by the blur of my tears
我可以通过我眼泪的模糊加倍

- After the Fall -
- 秋天之后 -

When I look back, the Garden is a dream to me
当我回首往事时,花园对我来说是一个梦想
It was beautiful, surpassingly beautiful, enchantingly beautiful
它美丽,超乎寻常的美丽,迷人的美丽
and now the garden is lost
现在花园消失了
and I shall not see it any more
我不会再看到它了

The Garden is lost, but I have found him
花园失落了,但我找到了他
and I am content with that
我对此感到满意
He loves me as well as he can
他尽其所能地爱我
I love him with all the strength of my passionate nature
我用我热情的天性的所有力量爱他
and this is proper to my youth and sex, I think
我认为这对我的青春和性是合适的
If I ask myself why I love him, I find I do not know
如果我问自己为什么爱他,我发现我不知道
and I do not really care to know
我真的不在乎知道
so I suppose this kind of love is not a product of reasoning
所以我想这种爱不是推理的产物
this love has nothing to do with statistics
这份爱与统计无关
it is different to the way one loves the animals
这与一个人爱动物的方式不同
I think that this must be so
我认为一定是这样
I love certain birds because of their song
我爱某些鸟,因为它们的歌声
but I do not love Adam on account of his singing
但我不爱亚当,因为他的歌声
No, it is not that
不,不是那样
the more he sings the more I do not get reconciled to it
他唱得越多我越不甘心
Yet I ask him to sing
然而我请他唱歌
because I wish to learn to like everything he is interested in
因为我希望学会喜欢他感兴趣的一切
I am sure I can learn
我相信我可以学习
because at first I could not stand it, but now I can

因为一开始我受不了了,但现在我可以
It sours the milk, but it doesn't matter
它使牛奶变酸,但没关系
I can get used to that kind of milk
我可以习惯那种牛奶

It is not on account of his brightness that I love him
我爱他不是因为他的聪明

no, it is not that
不,不是那样

He is not to blame for his brightness
他的聪明不应该怪他

because he did not make it himself
因为他不是自己做的

he is as God made him
他就像上帝创造他一样

and that is sufficient the way he is
他的方式就足够了

There was a wise purpose in it, that I know
我知道,这其中有一个明智的目的。

In time the purpose will develop
随着时间的推移,目的会发展

though I think it will not be sudden
虽然我认为这不会是突然的

and besides, there is no hurry
此外,不着急

he is good enough just as he is
他已经足够好了,就像他一样

It is not his grace for which I love him
我爱他的不是他的恩典

and I do not love him for his delicate nature
我不爱他,因为他的细腻本性

he would not be considerate for love either
他也不会为爱情着想

No, he is lacking in these regards
不,他缺乏这些方面

but he is well enough just as he is
但他已经足够好了,就像他一样

and he is improving
他正在进步

It is not on account of his industry that I love him
我爱他不是因为他的行业
No, it is not that
不,不是那样
I think he has it in him
我想他心里有
and I do not know why he conceals it from me
我不知道他为什么对我隐瞒
It is my only pain
这是我唯一的痛苦
Otherwise he is frank and open with me, now
否则他现在对我坦率和开放
I am sure he keeps nothing from me but this
我相信他没有对我隐瞒任何东西,除了这个

It grieves me that he should have a secret from me
我很难过,他应该对我保密

and sometimes it spoils my sleep thinking of it
有时想到它就会破坏我的睡眠

but I will put it out of my mind
但我会把它抛在脑后

it shall not trouble my happiness
它不会困扰我的幸福

my happiness is already almost overflowing
我的幸福已经快溢出来了

It is not on account of his education that I love him
我爱他不是因为他的教育

No, it is not that
不,不是那样

He is self-educated
他是自学成才的

and he does really know a multitude of things
他确实知道很多事情

It is not on account of his chivalry that I love him
我爱他不是因为他的骑士精神

No, it is not that
不,不是那样

He told on me, but I do not blame him
他告诉我,但我不怪他

it is a peculiarity of sex, I think
我认为这是性的一种特殊性

and he did not make his sex
而且他没有做爱

Of course I would not have told on him
我当然不会告诉他

I would have perished before telling on him
在告诉他之前,我会死的

but that is a peculiarity of sex, too
但这也是性的特点。

and I do not take credit for it
我不相信它

because I did not make my sex
因为我没有做爱
Then why is it that I love him?
那我为什么爱他呢？
MERELY BECAUSE HE IS MASCULINE, I think
仅仅因为他是男性，我认为

At bottom he is good, and I love him for that
在底下，他很好，我爱他
but I could love him without him being good
但我可以爱他，而他不好
If he beat me and abused me I could go on loving him
如果他打我，虐待我，我可以继续爱他
I know it is that way
我知道是这样
It is a matter of my sex, I think
我想这是我的性别问题
He is strong and handsome
他强壮而英俊
and I love him for that
我爱他
and I admire him
我很佩服他
and am proud of him
并为他感到骄傲
but I could love him without those qualities
但我可以爱他，没有这些品质
If he were plain, I would still love him
如果他是平淡的，我仍然会爱他
if he were a wreck, I would still love him
如果他是残骸，我仍然会爱他
and I would work for him
我会为他工作
and I would slave over him
我会奴役他
and I would pray for him
我会为他祈祷
and I would watch by his bedside until I died
我会在他的床边看着，直到我死去

Yes, I think I love him merely because he is MINE
是的，我想我爱他只是因为他是我的
and I love him because he is MASCULINE
我爱他，因为他是男性
There is no other reason, I suppose
我想没有其他原因
And so I think it is as I first said
所以我认为就像我第一次说的那样
this kind of love is not a product of reasoning and statistics
这种爱不是推理和统计的产物

this kind of love just comes by itself
这种爱就是自己来的
No one knows when it will come
没有人知道它什么时候会到来
and love cannot explain itself
爱无法解释自己
love doesn't need to explain itself
爱不需要解释自己
that is what I think, but I am only a girl
我就是这么想的,但我只是一个女孩
I am the first girl that has examined this matter
我是第一个研究这个问题的女孩
although, out of inexperience, I may not have gotten it right
虽然,由于缺乏经验,我可能没有做对

- Forty Years Later -
- 四十年后 -

It is my prayer, it is my longing;
这是我的祈祷,这是我的渴望;
I pray that we pass from this life together
我祈祷我们一起度过今生
this longing shall never perish from the earth
这种渴望永远不会从地球上消失
but it shall have place in the heart of every wife that loves
但它将在每个爱的妻子的心中占有一席之地
until the end of time
直到时间的尽头
and it shall be called by my name; Eve
它必以我的名呼召; 夏娃

But if one of us must go first, it is my prayer that it shall be I
但是，如果我们中的一个人必须先走，我祈祷这将是我
for he is strong, I am weak
因为他是坚强的，我是软弱的
I am not as necessary to him as he is to me
我对他不像他对我那样必要
life without him would not be life
没有他的生活就不是生活
how could I endure it?
我怎么能忍受呢？
This prayer is also immortal
这个祈祷也是不朽的
this prayer will not cease from being offered up while my race continues
当我的比赛继续时，这个祈祷不会停止被奉献
I am the first wife
我是第一任妻子
and in the last wife I shall be repeated
在最后的妻子中，我将重复

- At Eve's Grave -
- 在夏娃的坟墓 -

ADAM: "Wheresoever she was, there was Eden"
亚当:"无论她在哪里,哪里就有伊甸园"

www.ingramcontent.com/pod-product-compliance
Lightning Source LLC
Chambersburg PA
CBHW011952090526
44591CB00020B/2735